Catholic Daughters
of
Catholic Mothers

Catholic Daughters
of
Catholic Mothers

A Memoir and Guided Journal

Dr. Martha Lucas, L.Ac.

www.acupuncturewoman.com

ArmLin House, Inc.

ARMLIN HOUSE, INC.
P.O. Box 2522, Littleton, Colorado 80161-2522

ISBN: 978-1-958185-00-1

Cover Design by Dancing Tornado Designs
www.dancingtornado.com

Printed in the United States of America

FIRST EDITION

I dedicate this book to the memory of my Catholic mother,
Elsie Jean Braxtor Lucas.

.

A note to you, the reader:

I am *not* above the pain of being a Catholic daughter of a Catholic mother …. I'm in the thick of it. I write for myself as much as for you.

Dr. Martha

Contents

The Prebirth Naming Decision or Why Martha
    Became My Name   1

Projectile Vomiting: One of the Sources of My Catholic Guilt   5

Baptism: The Formal Naming Ceremony, the Initiation,
    the First White Dress   11

Catholic Grade School   15

Mass, Missals, and Mortal Sins   21

Confession   27

First Communion   33

Easter, Lent, Abstinence on Fridays, Hyper Vigilance,
    and Guilt   39

Confirmation   45

The Little Pink Period Book   49

Mom and Dad's Wedding Anniversary: The Origin of
    My Wanting Everything to Be Perfect   53

Clambakes and Bazaars   59

The Knights of Columbus and Catholic Daughters   63

Breasts Don't Hang Out in Our Family   67

Oops, Pregnant and Not Married   73

The Apology Letter   79

Raising My Children as Catholics   83

My D I V O R C E   89

Dating and Remarriage: To Annul or Not to Annul   95

When Did You Start to Become an Ambiguous Catholic?   99

Banned Books, Mom, and George   103

Death and Catholicism   109

What Now?   115

Introduction

ATHOLIC DAUGHTERS *of Catholic Mothers: A Memoir and Guided Journal* is a way for women to share experiences. The events in this book all happened and made me the person I am today. If you are reading this book, your girlhood womanhood, motherhood were and are affected by the religious force that was your mother.

I wrote the book so that you can read about, talk about, and write about your experiences with a Catholic mother too. It's an *heirloom product*. You will write your Catholic daughter experiences and then share them with your daughter(s) and so on. A shared understanding of what it has meant to be a Catholic daughter will come forward.

You'll cringe.

You'll laugh.

You'll relate.

You'll cry.

You'll celebrate.

You'll forgive.

You'll understand.

You'll grow.

I have had this book in my mind for years and now it is in yours.

The Prebirth Naming Decision or Why Martha Became My Name

THE BEGINNING of one's life can be a strange affair. Back in the day, when I was born, or pre-born, the rule among Catholics was to name children after saints. Just like nowadays, they planned ahead, but there wasn't much worry about trends—like in the 70s when we all named our girls Jennifer. Some families looked at their family trees. The fact was, if you were Catholic, the family tree probably had all saints' names on it anyway. But my father's dad ran away after he was born. I'm not sure anyone would want to name a male child after an ass like that. Otherwise, there was John, my mother's father, but naming the first son John was already a given since that was my Father's name. Our female family names were Mary (Mom's mother) and Rose (Dad's mother), a pretty name. One of my grands is named Violet, and everyone loves it. I could never have lived up to the name Mary—after the Blessed Mother—for Pete's sake. The pressure. But clearly my parents didn't choose either of those names for me.

They named me after Saint Martha, the patron saint of housewives, servants, and cooks. Catholics turn to her when dealing with chronic stress and doubt. Martha was a worker, keeping everybody fed and dressed in clean clothes, while her sister Mary had chosen "the good portion." What's meant by this old saying is that Mary was concerned

1

with more spiritual things. She was the sister who spent countless hours conversing with Jesus almost to the exclusion of practical and domestic matters that were more suitable burdens for Martha.

During my birth, my mother suffered through a very long and hard labor—I obviously didn't want to come out. A priest even gave her the last rites. My mother and father decided that if she lived and the child lived, and it was a girl, the child would be named Martha. A boy would be named John Jr., which was already a given. Well, it was me… Martha Lucas. It's the name they gave me and the name I've kept. Admittedly, I've changed it due to marriage even though the man to whom I am married now has the opinion, "why would you take my name? I don't own you. You are not my property."

Martha Lucas. It feels good somehow. It's who I am.

Your Turn

How did your parents decide your name? Are there stories about it?

What is your name's meaning?

Have you kept your original name?

Do you like it?

J✝MJ

Projectile Vomiting: One of the Sources of My Catholic Guilt

PPARENTLY I couldn't "stomach" my early life and so ruined my mother's first year of being a mother—the Catholic guilt of it all. *Guilt*. There it is! The *guilt* word. I made my mother's motherhood experience miserable, at least for that first year. Damn! Parenthood was supposed to be sweet. I was supposed to be an adorable, good girl not a vomiting screamer.

If you believe babies can sense stress, then I was a real champ at it. My parents didn't get along, and I could sense it. Babies do that. I was the first child born into the chaos of a dysfunctional marriage. There was a lot of stress in the home, and, according to my mother, I did a lot of screaming and vomiting—projectile vomiting. Exorcist-level stuff.

My parents didn't use birth control—off limits to Catholics back then—so there were more children to come. Maybe my parents tried the rhythm method, but the fact is that four more children came, rhythm or no rhythm. Mom used to tell me that my brother, who was born about 15 months after me, was the "sweetest baby ever" after dealing with me. The story is that all I did was scream and vomit, scream and vomit, and then came their first son. Three more boys were to come after that. Four boys and me were all born into a dysfunctional family; all five of us paid dearly for it.

5

One thing I have had issues with my entire life is self-soothing. It's how normal people calm themselves down when things get rough. But my brain, my "rat" brain as I call my amygdala, the brain's alarm bell in the limbic/emotional system of the brain, sets my alarm bells off for the simplest things. Clearly, it all started right after birth. I couldn't "stomach" the stress in the home. I must have been an awfully anxious little baby. And what does an anxious baby turn into? An anxious adult. I still deal with the fear of becoming a helpless poor kid again. That early childhood pattern of anxiety is the generator of my emergency, slip into fight or flight so that I'll survive, mode. I remember Mom frequently reminded us she was going to have to check into Our Lady of Peace. That was the local asylum. A kinder description would be the local rest home. I guess she was telling us she was on the verge of a nervous breakdown. Like mother, like daughter. When your mother fails to soothe you, it's difficult to learn how to soothe yourself. It's not a skill that comes with being born.

Granted, I didn't ask for soothing much. Guess I learned early on that I wasn't going to get it. My sense is that when you are unconditionally loved, you don't need to ask for soothing: hugging, kissing on the forehead, rubbing your back. I *think* those are all parts of being unconditionally loved by your mother. My mother was trying to save herself and then four brothers after me. She didn't have it in her. My therapist asked me once why I didn't tell my mother that I got up every night after she went to bed to wait for my dad to come home. You know, in the moment, ask her to comfort me in my fear that Dad would die in a drunk driving accident. I answered, "You're kidding me. I *never* even thought of doing that because she would have yelled at me for getting up." I don't feel like she had it inside her to soothe me or even sit on the steps with me. What a dream that would have been… to have Mom and me sitting together waiting for Dad to come home. A unit. A scared child being loved and supported by her mother. No. That wouldn't have happened. I would have just gotten in trouble.

I did try once in my thirties to tell my mom that I didn't feel like she loved me. She, of course, was shocked. She asked me how I could feel that way when she used to read to me every night, although I have *no* memory of her doing so. She just couldn't fathom that I felt unloved. Naturally, how would any of us mothers feel if our children told us they didn't think we loved them? It would hurt, probably put us on the defensive. What happened after my confession was what was most interesting to me. After our conversation, Mom sent a letter or a package to me, and she addressed it to "Dr. Martha Lucas." *Her* way of showing love was by acknowledging that I *am* a doctor. It still makes me smile, in a sad smile way, when I think about those letters. And sad for her that she had been reduced to not being able to hug her children, or to cry with her daughter about the past. I mean bawl about it—really share our love. I'd prefer to think I have that kind of relationship with my daughters—and son for that matter. But I took what I could get.

Your Turn

How did your mother describe you as a baby?

Where were you in the birth order?

Was your mother ready to mother you?

Do you or did you feel nurtured and loved by your mother?

Baptism: The Formal Naming Ceremony, the Initiation, the First White Dress

W E DON'T remember it, but we all have pictures and stories about it: our baptism. It was the beginning of our formal journey into Catholicism. Our initiation. It was our time of regeneration, our repentance, our first forgiveness of sins. *But what sins?* That's what I'd like to know, even though we are all aware of the Catholic answer—our *original* sins. This is the time we wear our first white dress, the baptismal gown, to signify our transformation from having sin to not having sin.

Our baptism is the first time that our name is called out to God and our first meeting with the Father, the Son, and the Holy Ghost (aka Holy Spirit) via the attending priest's words, "I baptize you in the name of the Father, and of the Son, and of the Holy Ghost."

Our parents weren't required to name us after a saint, but they were strongly advised to. And they were expected to avoid names that go against Catholic sensibility. Names that have a negative connotation such as *Satan* or *Lucifer* or *Beelzebub*—my brothers' nicknames for our father. However, believe it or not, if the priest didn't like a parent's choice for a name, he could intervene. Yeah, he could refuse to do the ceremony.

Supposedly, naming one's child after a saint reaffirms commitment to your faith. Everyone hoped that as we grew older, we would be curious and learn more about our namesake, and that would confirm *our* faith even more. Martha was a housewife while her sister Mary flitted around with Jesus Christ, leaving Martha behind to do housework. That's what I learned about my namesake… just saying.

Our namesake saint was also someone who was easy for us to remember to pray to in times of stress. It was easy to just call out our own name and pray. *St. Martha, help me!* That would have been my prayer.

The whole which-saint-to-pray-to thing is still interesting to me. I have Blessed Mary candles, St. Jude candles, and Holy Spirit candles. They've gotten me through some tough times.

When I just want comfort, it's Mary.

When I need a miracle, it's St. Jude.

When I or someone I love needs guidance, knowledge, or help with decisions, it's the Holy Spirit.

And I feel like they come through for me!

I don't remember ever looking for a St. Martha candle. So, guess what? While writing this book, I decided to see if there even *are* St. Martha candles. It turns out they exist! Finding that out didn't make me want to purchase one, but now I know they are available in case I ever need to call out, *St. Martha, please help me!* I feel a little guilty that I don't want to buy one.

Sigh. Catholic Guilt.

Your Turn

Did your parents choose a saint's name for you, or did they break the rules?

Was your namesake your favorite "go to" when praying during times of stress?

Catholic Grade School

OR GRADE school, I went to St. John the Evangelist Catholic School, located in my hometown, Wilkes Barre, Pennsylvania. I started there in second grade, after we moved up to "the Boo" from Philly when I was about seven.

At St. John's I wore one of those red, white, and black plaid uniforms. My skirt was never above the knee. According to my mother, one inch below the knee was the only appropriate length. No boy was going to see my underwear. Modesty was the word of the day… every day. In fact, I never saw my mother in less than underwear and a full slip, and that was behind her bedroom door when I entered uninvited. She hid behind the door, trying to cover herself up. No skin hung out in our home. It's funny the things you remember. Especially since I normally experience childhood amnesia. I was in my thirties before I realized that my mother stating, "Your butt is hanging out of your bathing suit." was a commentary about exposing skin, *not* about being fat. Yes, when you wear a bathing suit, your butt is out there. But when you weigh 98 pounds and think you're fat, the message came from somewhere. Mom. My body image issues were all falsely based on the memory that my mother had a waist when she brought my youngest brother home from the hospital, but afterward she was obese. Like it happened in an instant. That memory led me to feel out of control about weight because of her message that you can be thin one day and obese the next. Insight on issues like that hopefully comes to us so we're not stuck in old, unproductive, anxiety producing emotional patterns for longer than we have to be.

Then there were the nuns. My husband went to an all-boys boarding school, and he likes to tell a story about Sister Mary Jude. He says she could write on the blackboard, hear a commotion happening behind her, whip around, and hit a boy right between the eyes with an eraser. I don't remember our nuns having skills like that, but there's one thing in particular from grade school that has fixed the way I continue to respond to sirens for over 50 years. During class one day in 5th grade, a nun entered the classroom and whispered something into Sister Geraldine's ear, who then told us to take a moment to say a Hail Mary. We all moaned and groaned about having to do it but joined in the prayer. Well, it turned out that one of my classmate's father had died on the way to the hospital. Yep, died in an ambulance. Naturally, I felt super guilty for complaining about having to take a minute and say a Hail Mary. There's that Catholic guilt again. So I've been making up for that moaning ever since. Today, I can't hear a siren—ambulance or not—without saying a Hail Mary. These days I also do long distance Reiki for the victims, but that's another story. One of my daughters told me she does the same thing when she hears a siren: another true Catholic daughter of a Catholic mother.

> *Hail Mary, full of Grace,*
> *The Lord is with thee.*
> *Blessed art thou among women*
> *and blessed is the fruit of thy womb, Jesus.*
> *Holy Mary, Mother of God,*
> *pray for us sinners*
> *now and at the hour of our death.*
> *Amen.*

A friend once told me that after she and her family moved from Pennsylvania to Kentucky, a priest found out that she was a Catholic going to a public school. He told her, "In Kentucky, if you're Catholic, you go to Catholic school." *Isn't that crazy?* But he scared the heck out of her, and the next thing she knew, she and her brother were in Catholic grade school. She said she spent a lot of time sitting in the corner because she hated that school. I also couldn't wait to leave Catholic school. When I won a full scholarship to the local all-girls Catholic high school, it devastated me. I *cried* and *cried* and *cried*. Frankly, I don't know how I did it, but I convinced my parents to let me attend the public high school, Coughlin, instead of St. Mary's. I wish I could remember because I'd be the world's greatest salesperson or persuader. So, St. John's was the last Catholic school for me.

Your Turn

Did you go to Catholic grade school?

How about high school or maybe college too?

What is your favorite memory of Catholic grade school?

What is your least favorite memory of Catholic grade school?

Mass, Missals, and Mortal Sins

W E WERE Roman Catholic, so back in the days when I was a kid, Mass was recited in Latin. Jesus Christ delivered the very first Mass at the Last Supper, where he told his followers to repeat the process to commemorate his death. According to some stories I was told, the Holy Spirit intervened and the Roman Catholic Mass was born. Some called it *Traditional Latin Mass* or *Classical Mass*. I called it *a pain*. To be fair, I've gone up and down on this over the years. I've spent many a moment in Mass as an adult crying and wishing that it felt "right" to be there. I'll always be a Catholic, what my husband calls an "ambiguous Catholic" due to my nonparticipation in the ceremonies. I call myself "spiritual." I believe in God (or someone), pray, and attend Mass sometimes, for special occasions or when I'm feeling depressingly lost. And I love paging through old missals: there's something about the feel of the onionskin paper. My favorite missal is one that my father owned. It contains our Philadelphia address written in his handwriting. We lived there for a few years before moving to Wilkes Barre. One bookmark in it is a picture of me that looks like I was maybe two years old. On the back, in my Dad's post-stroke scrawl, are some of our names, all in caps:

> MARTHA
> JOHNNY (with the Ns backward)
> JERRY
> ELSIE
> JOHN (Dad himself I guess)
> GERARD (Jerry again)

No space left on the back of the picture for my brothers Chris and Richard, I guess. But it could also have been that his stroke-addled brain put his name, Mom's name, and then double John, and that was all he could do. Those post-stroke years were sad, *very* sad. It was hard to see my father destroyed like that.

Anyway, back to the *Latin Mass*, where naturally, in the beginning, I had no idea what was happening. But faithfully, I tried to follow what was going on using one of the many red missals placed in every pew. I performed all the postures: sitting, standing, and kneeling. All done at the appropriate times, following what I was told to do and what other people were doing.

There was Mass etiquette too. The Powers That Be mandated that women had to wear a head covering during Mass, or in any church for that matter. It was the perfect sign of submission. The head covering was one sign that a woman wanted to humble herself before God. If you couldn't tell by now, I was the rebellious sort, sometimes showing up at Mass without a veil, or *mantilla*, or a hat. Mom would make me put a tissue on my head. If we didn't have a bobby pin to secure it, she would wet it with spit to paste it on my hair. Fun times.

I asked my daughters for any lessons that I, *their* Catholic mother, taught them, and Jennifer mentioned the fasting for an hour before Communion. Oh, the machinations we went through, trying to figure out the timing of Communion so we could eat or drink exactly an hour before we thought Communion would be offered. We couldn't just abstain from eating after 8 a.m. if it was a 9 a.m. Mass. We knew there would be various parts of the Mass before Communion and those took minutes. Naturally, if one would start the fast an hour before the actual Mass's starting time, thereby extending your fast, that was praiseworthy. We were supposed to be *hungry for the Lord*. Oh boy. I think we were even restricted from chewing gum because the flavor or sugar would break the fast.

I believe we were told that breaking the fast before Communion, and then receiving Communion was a mortal sin. Those things were scary. If you had a non-confessed mortal sin on your soul and you died, you went straight to Hell. No stopping at Go, no three strikes and you're out, no hiatus in Purgatory, you were going straight to Hell. It was a well-known fact that missing Mass was a mortal sin. Miss Mass on a Sunday or holy day—straight to hell. The theory is that you intentionally cut yourself away from God's grace by knowingly committing a mortal sin. Afterall, they gave us the list of mortal sins, so *we knew*. And God *knew* if we committed one. But there was an out, and it was called the Act of Contrition.

> *O my God, I am heartily sorry for having offended Thee, and I detest all my sins because of thy just punishments, but most of all because they offend Thee, my God, who art all good and deserving of all my love.*
>
> *I firmly resolve with the help of Thy grace to sin no more and to avoid the near occasion of sin. Amen.*

Saying the Act of Contrition was a way to fix our relationship with God—much like you would admit to a wrongdoing to a friend—apologize and promise to try harder not to commit the transgression again. I have actual memories of reminding myself that, if the plane I was on went down, I could say the Act of Contrition to resolve my mortal sins and be fine. I wouldn't go straight to hell. You can't believe how fast you can say it! Go ahead—try it for yourself. See how fast you can say it.

Your Turn

What kind of head covering did you wear to Mass?

Were you faithful with the hour-long fast before Communion, or did you ever *cheat* and receive Communion even though you didn't fast?

How long did it take you to say the Act of Contrition?

Confession

YOU REMEMBER Confession? I know you do. It was when you made up sins every week. You were seven or eight years old the first time.

In the name of the Father, the Son, and the Holy Spirit bless me Father, for I have sinned. This is my first confession.

But you had... *committed no sins*. You were not a sinner. Still, you went to confession every week so you would be pure for attending Mass on Sunday.

Actually, like me, you went because your parents took you or told you to go. In the eyes of the Church it was so that you would be pure enough to attend Mass. I apologize if you are the person who went because you loved the Mass. Hey, I love the choir; I love to sing; I love the feel of the onion paper in the Missal. *But...* it doesn't feel like home. I cry through most of Mass these days. So, I don't go very often.

Besides being pure enough to attend Mass, there's the belief that the confession of all serious sins is necessary after baptism. You had to confess them to the priest to receive absolution and keep that soul of yours clean. The priest was the healer. Funny... until I wrote those words, I never thought of a priest as a healer. But that was their role as the confessor: the healer of souls.

Before we could receive the sacrament of First Confession, we had to be able to tell the difference between right and wrong as well as understand what a sin was. Oh my… what kind of responsibility was this to put on a 6- or 7-year-old kid?

Obviously, our parents taught us right from wrong. But sin? How is a 6-year-old child supposed to understand an esoteric idea like sin: the sort of act that was wrong in the eyes of God. Wasn't it bad enough that we did something that our parents didn't want us to do or that *they* told us was wrong? No, we had to be concerned about what the eyes of God thought about us. One of my friends told me he was in his twenties before he convinced himself that God wasn't watching him all the time. Or worse, that his dead father wasn't seeing everything he did. Oh my. We all did that, I think. I used to be weirded out by the idea that my mother could see me do stuff from Heaven. There I was having sex out of wedlock, and Mom was watching. Yuck. How could I do anything without feeling weird?

No wonder we admit to doing things wrong during confession. Someone was always watching. The eyes of God were on us. I'll probably go to Hell for writing this book.

Writing this chapter brings a poem written by Barbara Drake to mind. It's a beloved little poem that my husband and I have enjoyed and smiled about for years because it's such a perfect reflection of how we felt during our First Confession. Besides reading her work, when we lived in McMinnville, I took some of Barbara's writing courses. I remember especially liking the "overheard conversations," where we transcribed conversations we heard while out and about town. It was fun, and I still think about doing it, maybe even writing a book of overheard conversations. I worked at a shelter for homeless men at the time and overheard some beauties between men and the unseen.

The poem, "First Confession," from her book *What We Say to Strangers* is perfect for this chapter.

> *The road to hell*
> *is paved with good intentions,*
> *said Sister Maria Theresa.*
> *What a spot I was in.*
> *At six, I had nothing*
> *but good intentions.*

Your Turn

Does this poem reflect how you felt about First Confession?

What kinds of sins did you make up when you were a kid just so you'd have something to say to the priest in that confessional booth?

Did you count how many sins you felt were *needed* to sound realistic?

What were your penances? Hail Marys? Our Fathers?

First Communion

BEFORE WE could receive First Communion, we had to reach the age of reason and properly prepare to receive the body of Christ. I guess it was on our parents to make certain we met both qualifications. One of the first requirements was that we had received the Sacrament of Penance or our first confession. I think I was seven years old and in 2nd grade when I received First Communion. Believe it or not, I think the "age of reason" part was when *they*—the powers that be—thought we could determine the difference between the Eucharist, the body and blood of Christ, the Lord's body and regular bread. I know, *really?* It's crazy to think that a 7- or 8-year-old child *could* understand the giant leap from "this is a piece of flattened bread and some wine" to "this is me receiving the body and blood of Christ with faith and devotion."

I had no idea that I was being invited to the table of the Lord. For me, getting First Communion was just another thing I had to do because I was being raised a Catholic. You can probably tell by the cover photo how excited I was about the glorious celebration.

Anyway, there was no way around it. I was going to receive the Holy Sacrament of First Communion whether or not I wanted it. And saying that I didn't want it was something that would never ever come out of my mouth. Why? Because my opinion wouldn't have mattered.

My parents hoped I would feel as if I was at the Last Supper myself, sharing a feast with Jesus and his friends. And because the host and wine represent his body and blood, he would be a part of *me*.

The priest would say:

> *Lord Jesus Christ, bless these children coming forward to receive Holy Communion for the first time. Thank you for their innocence and goodness.*
>
> *May this step they take today be a step toward a lifelong love of the Eucharist. Give them a hunger for this holy food so that they come to you for comfort and wisdom as they continue their discipleship.*
>
> *May their hands, extended to receive your body and blood, inspire us all to cherish this sacrament.*

My husband's Catholic upbringing continued through high school at a Jesuit boarding school. So, his training in the Latin Mass was much more rigorous than mine. He not only was an altar boy at Mass every morning, but he had to say the Mass in Latin. I just listened when I was a kid at Mass. While writing this chapter, he reminded me about *hoc est corpus*, which means *this is my* body in Latin. These are the words the priest says as he elevates the host toward heaven during the Consecration. Some say that those holy words are the origin of *hocus pocus*: the gibberish words that magicians and kids recite to provoke magical results. For all I remember, I could have thought that's what the priest was saying.

So, as I said previously, this is a crazy thing for a 7-year-old to contemplate. Weird ideas. But the fact is, every Sunday during my childhood, I received Communion. I still do when I go to the occasional Mass. I can accept symbolism as an adult and consider Communion a blessing of sorts, so I'm happy to take it when I'm at Mass. Apparently though, the Conference of Catholic Bishops has discovered that most Catholics do *not* understand what the Eucharist is, so they wrote a document called *The Mystery of the Eucharist in the Life of the Church* in 2021. Do you know how many times in my life, in my childhood alone, I watched the priest hold up the host and chalice and say, "The body and blood of Christ" to the members of the parish? Maybe people weren't listening and had tuned out by that part of the Mass, or they just didn't get it. This is unbelievable to me, but the bishops stated that people frequently ask, "When the bread and wine become the body and blood of Christ, why do they still look and taste like bread and wine?" This makes me cringe. No wonder they felt like they had to write a document explaining the meaning of the Eucharist.

There is one thing about Communion that I guess I should think about—uh oh, here comes some guilt—and that is how many Masses I've missed (*a lot*) before the one in which I'm currently attending and receiving Communion. Missing Mass is a mortal sin and not confessing this fact before you *do* go to Mass is another mortal sin. Compounded by the number of missed Masses, and that's a lot of mortal sins. *Oy.* I resolve that issue by believing that God is not counting mortal sins to decide "you come to Heaven" or "you go to Hell." I am at Mass because I need to talk with God or need some sort of support or insight. I believe God is happy to see me, and all is forgiven. Fingers crossed. And besides, I still remember the Act of Contrition.

Your Turn

Did you receive First Communion?

How did you feel about it? Were you excited? Did you understand what you were getting into?

Do you remember your dress… maybe even still have it or passed it on to your daughter(s)?

Did you then receive Communion every week at Mass? Do you receive it now?

Easter, Lent, Abstinence on Fridays, Hyper Vigilance, and Guilt

YEP, ALL of that was the experience of the Easter season for us Catholics. The season of Easter, or Lent, required days of fasting and abstinence to prepare our souls for the celebration of Easter Sunday. We knew that the sins would pile on if we weren't vigilant about things like abstinence and fasting. I still get struck by momentary guilt when one of my daughters reminds me on some random Friday during Lent that I ate meat. *Sigh.*

The word *Lent* has multiple meanings, and somehow it came to mean the forty days before Easter Sunday beginning on Ash Wednesday. One explanation is that the 40 days represent the 40 days and 40 nights that Jesus Christ spent fasting in the desert. There was also this tradition—the only word I can think to describe it because it wasn't a rule—of giving up something for Lent. It was supposed to be a sacrifice: an offering from me to God in exchange for blessings or grace. We Catholics always wanted more grace. I seem to have some vague memory that having enough grace was a way to cancel out the bad stuff and save one from Hell. Another possibility was that our giving up something may have been because Christ fasted for 40 days, and 40 nights and therefore you could give up *one thing* for 40 days. The sacrifice was in giving up something that you value. You don't give up spinach or finishing homework. Kids would give up candy or soda or maybe watching their favorite TV show during Lent. These days, I suppose kids could give up using electronics. As my children got older, I suggested that rather than giving up something—which usually was pretty silly anyway—that they would *give* something. They could volunteer somewhere or give away the things that they no longer needed or wanted. It made more sense to me to help the community.

Fasting was only supposed to be imposed on adults over 18 and abstinence over age 14. But guess what? That didn't apply in the Lucas household, where we were all in it together. To be fair, I don't remember Mom and Dad forcing us to fast except for that hour before Communion—hardly a fast by today's standards. But the abstinence thing… that was for everyone. During Lent, no meat on Friday was the rule we all had to follow. I heard no one refer to me as a *mackerel snapper*, but that was an old old, maybe from the 1800's, pejorative name some people called Catholics because of our ban on eating meat on Fridays.

We used to buy this absolutely beautiful fried fish every Friday, so I actually looked forward to Fridays during Lent. That fish with tons of fresh lemon squirted on top was so delicious. One thing I miss about Wilkes Barre is Valley Seafood. Yes, fish was permitted because it is a different category of animal than cows, chickens, sheep… The issue was making certain you didn't eat meat during the rest of day: no bacon for breakfast, no salami sandwich at lunch. You had to be aware and plan ahead or suffer the guilt of making a misstep. Another sin on my soul because I ate meat on Fridays during Lent. It's funny that it wasn't a sin in the usual sense of the word: that you had sinned against God. It was that you disobeyed what the Church was asking you to do. You were disobedient to those who were trying to keep you on the holy straight and narrow. *Oh my.*

Interesting, over the years, how much of the religion has been removed from the major Catholic holidays. At least for us "ambiguous Catholics." I still put up a manger scene at Christmas and have given all my grandchildren some form of manger or birth of Christ storybook at one time or another. But for Easter, it's been all about the fun of egg dyeing and Easter baskets. My bad. I'm not alone in this though. Easter parades, Easter eggs, Easter candy, all the fun stuff have

been around since the 1700s. Here's a little-known factoid about Easter candy that I've learned over the years while teaching Chinese medicine in Turkey. It turns out that jellybeans, some say, have their origin all the way back to a Biblical version of Turkish Delight.

But no excuses. It's my Catholic duty to pass on the religious aspect of the holiday. I'm lucky that 2 of 3 of my children and their children have lived near me, so we can gather for an Easter meal. At that meal, I am always very clear to express gratitude for our family and our blessings. Although all of that is wonderful, I think it's been a while since I mentioned that Easter Day is about celebrating the resurrection of Christ. Guilty.

Your Turn

Do you remember not eating meat on Fridays during Lent?

Did your family extend that to every Friday?

Was there a fish or vegetable dish that your family ate in the place of meat? What was it and did you love it?

Confirmation

THIS IS the ritual that means we are ready to accept the responsibility of our faith. Really, at 11, 12, or even younger, I was supposed to be ready to accept the responsibility of my faith? This was the time for us, like with all the sacraments, to receive more grace from God. Here we once again meet up with the Father, Son, and Holy Ghost. The name we choose for ourselves is supposed to be a saint's name: one who has the virtues we feel we possess or aspire to possess.

Here's what I remember about Confirmation. I was 11 or 12 and had found two adult women to befriend. They lived close by, so finding them didn't require much searching. Doris had bright red, curly hair and lived three doors away in a tiny apartment in a big, beautiful, old house, where I spent a lot of time. She introduced me to another woman with completely white and wispy hair, whom I called Aunt Kate. I have fond memories of going to Aunt Kate's house, three doors down from ours and in the opposite direction of Doris' apartment. She would make cocoa with hot water, and we would sip our drinks and eat little coffee cakes. They were Hostess, I think. I loved the time I spent with Doris and Aunt Kate.

Some would consider it strange for a young kid to be at these older ladies' houses, but I got away with it. Remember, by then Mom had four more kids to deal with, and my youngest brother was a baby. Add the alcoholic husband and not-very-present father, and her plate was full. No need to pay much attention to the perfect straight As daughter. That sucked, Mom. I could have used some love and attention rather than getting reprimanded for not practicing the piano enough. My guess is that I felt loved and safe with Doris and especially Aunt Kate.

Who doesn't like a little old lady who makes you cocoa and gives you sweets to eat? I don't even remember what we used to talk about, but I spent as much time as I was allowed with each of them.

Anyway, I wanted to take Doris as my Confirmation name. But it was unacceptable for my parents because it was not a saint's name. There were arguments, but I wasn't going to win. I ended up being forced to take my grandmother Braxtor's name, Mary. I was angry, hurt, powerless. That Confirmation Day was the only time in my life that I ever used the name Mary. As far as I know, there is no legal record of it. My name is still just Martha Lucas, NMI, no middle initial.

Now I ponder, *what was the point of Confirmation?* Well, it was one sacrament that Catholics needed to accomplish before progressing to one of the next sacraments, like marriage. It was a ritual that I had to go through because I was a Catholic daughter.

Your Turn

Did you receive Confirmation?

What name did you take? Do you still have it now?

If you have children, have they received Confirmation, and did you help them choose their Confirmation name?

The Little Pink Period Book

THIS IS how I learned about menstruation. I woke up one day and there was a little pink book about menstruation on my dresser. My mother was not going to say the word "vagina" or "uterus" or talk about sex in any way shape or form. There was no talk about sex or sexual organs in our house. Well, my mother did tell me, over and over again, that "men are disgusting." I guess her main message was to tell me to stay away from men. But, Mom, blood would start coming out of my body! Your little girl would start bleeding, probably be scared about it, and you couldn't talk about it for God's sake? At least try to help me understand that all is well; all is normal when I start my menses. You needed to put your big-girl pants on and say "vagina." Nope. All she cared about was getting that "men are disgusting" message across. It wasn't until I was a much older teenager that I was able to say, albeit meekly, "Mom, not *all* men are disgusting."

We never talked about having a period, having sex, where babies come from. None of that. Oh, I'm wrong. She told me that using tampons was wrong because it would break my hymen, and I wouldn't be a virgin anymore. Yeah, *that* was important. I was so afraid of that happening and didn't really know anything about tampons because I would never try them after her warning. Well, not until I was on our high school graduation trip and started my period. The only tool available was, yes, you guessed it, a tampon from a friend. Naturally, I never went back to pads after that. A tampon stole my virginity.

When I think back on all these memories, they seem so ridiculous. *Breaking the hymen.* The whole *virgin* thing and the importance of it. Being afraid to say, or for Mom, probably more embarrassed to say the word "vagina." Or her inability to tell me about how intercourse works. I had *no* idea. Mom's only message was the "men are disgusting" one, and Dad's was "keep your legs crossed." And he told the boys, "Keep it in your pants." It makes me cringe to think about those instructions. *Crude.*

After growing up with that crap, I was determined to use biologically correct words when discussing bodily functions with my children. There is nothing wrong with talking about body parts and using their "real" names. I even told my girls to look at the guy's penis for things like herpes sores. They both were like, "Mom! *Ewwww.*" My response, "What… you're going to let him put it in your body without looking at it!" Eye rolls from them.

I also let my children see me naked, up to a certain age of course. I guess *that* can be considered crude, but I was determined that we were going to be free with our bodies, know how they work, and not be embarrassed by them. I wanted them to know about all the body parts and how they worked, and especially to love their bodies. It was still difficult for my daughters because even when I weighed 98 pounds, I somehow projected the message that I was fat. My body image issue projected onto my daughters even though I didn't want it to. It's sad because you just want your girls to love themselves and love their bodies. That's one thing I feel guilty or bad about in terms of the messages I sent, even if inadvertently, to my children. Another thing to work on in therapy.

Your Turn

How did your mother introduce you to your period? Or didn't she?

Did she talk with you about sex and how intercourse works?

Was the "feeling fat" thing just my mom's mis-messaging or did you get an idea like that too?

Mom and Dad's Wedding Anniversary: The Origin of My Wanting Everything to Be Perfect

CTUALLY, I should say the origin of my *needing* everything to be perfect. And the origin of my anxiety about everything *needing* to be perfect.

Oh my, how I wanted to fix my parent's marriage. Even though it was clear to us kids that our parents didn't have a loving relationship, and I knew their relationship was nothing to celebrate, I gave them a card on their wedding anniversary. When I was old enough, I baked a cake for the occasion. To be fair, my father was an alcoholic, and he hardly ever came home for dinner because he was at "the club" drinking with his buddies. So, there was good reason for Mom to be angry. I guess what I'm trying to say is that it wasn't like we had a *Leave to Beaver* life, and my mother wasn't a naturally bitter woman who ignored or disliked my father. Like I said, she had reason to be upset. The thing is, they used to party before they got married—whatever *that* meant in the early 1950's—so she knew Dad liked to drink. But how many women think a man will change, that his behavior will magically improve, that he'll give up all his "bad" habits after the wedding day? Lots! Lots and lots of women make that mistake. Mom was just one of them.

It didn't matter. I so wanted them to be happy and did what I could in my little-girl power to fix them. And, you know, I don't remember ever once getting a thank you. Dad most likely didn't even come home for dinner those nights, so he didn't even know about the cakes or the cards. Probably just unwittingly putting salt in their wounds. But I so wanted them to be happy. I wanted them to have the perfect "I love you" relationship. How did I even know about such a thing? But it's what I wanted. Maybe my true thinking was, if they loved and nurtured each other, then we kids would get some of it.

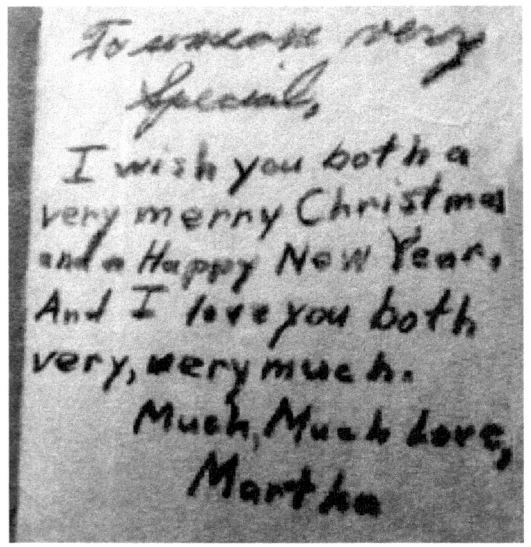

So, I planned and drew and baked, hoping that my perfect gift would make it all better. But no matter how "perfect" I thought it all was, nothing was good enough. Not by a long shot. Their anniversary day was probably sadder for me than it was for them because I made an effort and got nothing in return. Nothing.

Unfortunately, now I want everything to be perfect for everyone! Mom and Dad are gone, but there are plenty of other people to witness the perfection in my efforts. For example, if all the food on the Thanksgiving dinner table is not the same temperature when I serve it, I feel awful and apologize because it's not perfect. Since pretty much nothing is perfect, you can imagine that I spend a lot of time apologizing. I think that my children are catching on because this year I tried something new: rib roast. Compliments all around and when I chastised myself out loud for not having it as warm as the rest of the food—or some other ridiculous thing—my son said, "Mom, it's perfect. I mean it. It tastes great… the best thing ever." *Aww.* Thank you so much son for noticing my effort.

Catholics didn't get divorced when I was a kid. At least that's what Mom said. No divorce allowed. You're married in the eyes of God, and you stay married no matter what. I don't think that's how it works. I think God allows divorce, but there may be some rules about remarriage or getting your marriage annulled before you get remarried. Whatever the rules, Mom wasn't going to do it. Maybe she was afraid. She didn't have a job and first there was one child, then there were two children, then three, then four, then five! She had her master's degree in Music and was a talented musician and teacher, but she didn't have a job. After my youngest brother went to grade school, she went to work as a music teacher. So, at thirteen or fourteen years into what some would call a "bad" marriage, maybe it just seemed easier to her to wait it out. Wait until all the kids left home for college was maybe her thinking.

She did leave my dad once. It was so bizarre. He had a major stroke and was left paralyzed on the right side. He was in the hospital, then rehab, and before he moved home, Mom moved out. We couldn't believe it! Call it bad timing, but why now? Why didn't you do this 20 years ago? Anyway, Dad had to return home and be by himself. God, it was sad. And I was, frankly, angry with my mother. I felt like, *Really, now is the time you decide to leave, when Dad actually needs someone?* But it must have been hard to face up to caring for someone that you basically hate. And not only that, "men are disgusting" was what Mom had to be thinking the whole time, and now she had a more or less disabled "disgusting" man to take care of. Her living away lasted a couple of months. She said she was afraid to live alone. Mom, you lived in Wilkes Barre. What was there to be afraid of? Dad sits in a chair all day, has to use a walker to get around, and he's going to protect you? But that was that. She was back in the house. I didn't live there then, so I didn't get the pleasure of what the day to day must have been like. I think Mom helped Dad out with food. In other words, she may have gotten something ready for him before she left the house to volunteer at the local pro-life center. She spent as much time as she could out of the house, rescuing herself.

What a thing for children to watch, even adult children. It was hell watching her play the role of what I call the "angry housewife" in a tongue in cheek way. Constant angry housewife. It was another lesson for who I didn't want to be as an adult woman. Sad because I think, in general, kids sort of want to be like their parents, don't they? I was the opposite. Mom was everything I didn't want to be. So sorry to say that, Mom. I didn't want to be unhappily married, unable to nurture my children, overweight and hating my body, and generally just miserably angry and unhappy. What a sad waste of a life. Waste is too strong a word because of that old cliché—I wouldn't be here and who I am without them—but you know what I mean.

Your Turn

Did you feel like your parents had a happy marriage?

Do you remember their wedding anniversary date?

Was it a happy day in your family's life?

JMJ

Clambakes and Bazaars

O UR CHURCH, like most Catholic churches or parishes, had a few annual events to raise money and get the flock together. One such event was the clambake. They were grand, outside gatherings with lots of food and beer. I don't remember them having actual bars where you could purchase or exchange a ticket for a drink other than beer. Probably because Dad's drink of choice was beer, so that was my focus in the world of alcohol. I used to love the food at these events. But the event would always turn into the women and families leaving while the men stayed and drank. Another night wondering if Dad would come home alive or die in a drunk driving accident.

You know, Dad never missed a day of work because of his drinking. Not one. But he didn't come home after work, not for dinner, not for tucking us in before bed. So, every night, I would read by the light that came into my room from under my bedroom door and wait for Mom to go to bed. When she did, I would sneak down onto the stairs leading up to our second floor, avoiding the creaky steps, and sit there, looking down the steps to the street below, waiting for Dad to walk up. We lived up on a hill, and I had to go up a long flight of stairs to get to the house. So, I could see the street and the stairs up the driveway from our inside stairs. When I saw Dad come up the steps from his car, I could go to bed knowing that he was alive. Every night as a kid, I worried about the worst possible outcome: a parent dying. No wonder fear has been my "go to" emotion for most of my adult life. Fear of everything about loss: loss of income, loss of love (a *huge* one), loss of security, loss of respect, loss of home, along with a great fear of criticism, which probably equates to needing people to see my work as acceptable. The list goes on.

After I turned sixteen, I would bring Dad home from the clambakes because he was too drunk to drive. I was embarrassed by him.

The bazaar was the big moneymaker for the parish. I loved the bazaars. There was food, games, crafts to purchase, and a bake sale—so many homemade cookies, cakes, and pies. The event was just plain fun. Most of the time it would start out with a fish fry or other such meal on the Friday night before the weekend festivities. Sometimes there'd be a Sunday night meal at the end. The women would run the booths and the men would huddle around the barbecue grills or the makeshift bar. You know that game where you can try to toss a ring onto a bottle? We had that. Another had bottles stacked into pyramids that you tried to knock down. There was the ever-present Bingo and one of those wheels where you chose a number and hoped that the flapper thing would land on it. And all the fun was paid for with tickets. Those colored tickets with the numbers down the side were the currency of the day. I never won anything worth owning, but the fun was in meeting up with my friends, playing the games, and enjoying the smells and flavors of the food. As I got older, bazaars were mainly about the wandering around with friends.

My children remember bazaars. We lived in the rectory, yes, the rectory, at St. John Vianney Church in Louisville. Our next-door neighbors were the Sisters of Charity of Nazareth and I worked for the Senate of Religious. We were right in the middle of Catholicism. And that included Friday night fried fish and bazaars. I honestly don't know anyone who says they didn't enjoy going to a parish bazaar.

Your Turn

Did you belong to a parish?

Did you have clambakes or bazaars?

Did you even work at the bazaar? Which booth?

If not bazaars, how did your parish make money?

JMJ

The Knights of Columbus and Catholic Daughters

D AD BELONGED to the Knights of Columbus (K of C). It's a
fraternal organization open to practicing Catholic men. Father
Michael McGivney formed the K of C, and I once prayed to
him for a miracle. At the time, when I felt like I needed a miracle, I
found out that Fr. McGivney needed one more miracle assigned to
his case to be named a saint. Initially, I was praying to him to end the
pandemic, kill SARS Cov-2, give me my freaking life back. After I
thought about it though, it seemed it would be complicated to *prove*
that the pandemic ended due to one person and one act. And how
would the timeline work? Because it takes some days for the virus
to cook inside you, it would be impossible for a pandemic to be here
one day and gone the next. So, I gave that up… although here one
day, gone the next is the definition of miracle.

I revisited praying to Fr. McGivney when I felt like one of my children needed a healthcare miracle. Do you know how hard it is to pray
for a miracle? Trying to ask for what you actually want? Figuring out
the exact outcome that you want without making a mistake? It's crazy.
Plus, I was guilt-ridden that I, Martha Lucas, should be bold enough
to ask for a miracle. Who was I to ask for such a gift? Catholic guilt
weaves its way into every aspect of one's life, even into your prayer life.

Anyway, back to the K of C and the Catholic Daughters. Honestly, I don't remember a lot about being a Catholic Daughter of America (CDA). It is an affiliate of the K of C and both are charitable organizations that are involved in the community ostensibly to help families in need. The early CDA helped with the war effort during World War II. They sewed bandages, donated blood, and provided other sorts of support. Frankly, I have no memory of doing anything charitable. In fact, the absolutely only thing I remember about being a CDA is the debutante ball that was held by the K of C. I didn't want to attend; I didn't want to find a boy to ask to go; I didn't want any part of it. Naturally, that didn't matter. It was a done deal. My parents told me to ask a classmate of mine with good grades, although I couldn't imagine spending a minute of time with

him, let alone an entire evening, but he said, "yes." *Damn.* The look on my face in the First Communion picture on the cover of this book, well, that was my "I'm a debutante" look too. Another white dress—what's with all the white dresses for us Catholic girls? We all know the answer: we were clean and pure before God and ready for transformation. At the debutante ball, every girl was "presented" to the bishop by her father in an elaborate ceremony. We even did a group curtsey.

It was stupid. I hated everything about it. I thought the K of C was another place for Dad to go to drink with his buddies. There was no evidence that Dad was out doing good deeds or community service.

Your Turn

Did you belong to any Catholic girls' groups?

Did you do community service in the name of your parish?

Was your father a Knight of Columbus or maybe your mother was a Catholic Daughter?

Breasts and Butts Don't Hang Out in Our Family

MODESTY AND shame. Strangely, I think they go together or at least have gone together in my life. My mother's focus on modesty created a body image problem that still haunts me to this day. I can never be thin enough. Thank God that never translated into an eating disorder. It's just a daily worry about being fat: criticizing my body, wondering if I can weigh less, and distressing about ballooning into a fat blimp in a flash. One day I have a waist and the next I'm 100 pounds overweight. Kind of like what I said about my mother previously, having a waist after she had my youngest brother and then, before my eyes, she was fat. That's what I have told myself for more than 50 years. Intellectually, I know she didn't become overweight overnight, but the story I've told myself is exactly that. It happened in the blink of an eye. And so, I believe it can happen to me. The scale will just keep going up, and I won't be able to stop it. I must be vigilant. I was 10 years old when Mom had a waist. After that, all I remember is the overweight body. The body hidden in tent dresses.

There's a sense of shame of all things body related. But it's more than just shameful if I wear too short a skirt, or too low-cut a blouse, or too sexy a dress, or no bra in public. The not wearing a bra thing. You know why that will never happen, me being in public without a bra? Because when I was about 16 years old in the days of burning bras, I went to work one day without a bra. It just so happened that Mom came to the mall that day, saw me without a bra on, and made me ask my boss for a break so I could go *buy a bra*. Yep. That was her response. Not "Martha! Don't ever go out again without wearing a bra. And by the way, you're grounded for a week." Nope. It's always black or white… good or bad. She made me buy a bra and put it on before I went back to work. And I still think

about that episode of our life together. God, I hope I never made my girls feel that way, embarrassed and terrible about not wear- ing a piece of underwear. And the why of it. Why do I have to wear a bra? Because men, disgusting men, will see me as a sex object? Will going braless make me want to have sex? Are nipples a body part to be hidden? Will people think I'm a slut? Mom never explained why all those thoughts are in my mind when I don't wear a bra. God forbid our handyman should show up one day when I'm casual at home without a bra on. What would he think? "That's ridiculous," my intellectual brain says, but my rat brain says, "Don't do it."

Then there was the time I told Mom I was going to try out to be a strutter in high school. Maybe they're called pom pom girls today. We were a squad of girls, dressed in very short uniforms, whose undies matched our dresses, and we performed dance programs—well, strut- ting programs—during high school football games. I so wanted to be a strutter. Naturally, dancing around the football field, swishing our skirts up so our undergarments showed in front of hundreds of fans wasn't my mother's idea of good, wholesome fun. But I was determined. *And I would not let her lengthen my uniforms!* Oh my God… they were uniforms. One girl doesn't show up with a uniform down to her knees. Well, one inch below the knee was Mom's rule. They were cute too: all velveteen with furry white trimmings. So pretty. Anyway, after much arguing and threatening, I tried out and got on the squad. I was thrilled. I'll never forget a note I found from my Dad in a book that said, "GO STRUT!" on the day of tryouts. Warms my heart. Mom's reaction was, "If you get sick at all, one asthma attack during football season, you're off the squad." Guess what? I didn't have any asthma attacks during all of high school football seasons.

All those messages about hiding my body, my "private parts," and about not having any flesh showing, not only created body image issues but created an internal state of inadequacy no matter how hard I work. Unworthiness. I expect others see me as not smart enough… not successful enough. That's the big one, "successful enough." Whenever I look inward, try to see how I'm doing with life, how I look, whether I'm successful, it's with a very critical eye. I evaluate myself harshly and end up in a state of negative self-evaluation. That has all got to be rooted in childhood messages from Mom about my butt hanging out when I wore a bathing suit. It took me until I was in my middle to late thirties, I think, to figure that one out. On a visit home, for some reason, I decided to show my mom a new bathing suit I had bought and to ask her opinion. There's that wanting her approval, wanting her to notice me, wanting her to say something—anything—positive. It was love unreciprocated and my continuous struggle to get it from her.

A study that I recall from some time ago told mothers to have a straight face while their baby smiled and cooed and vied for the mother's attention. The babies ended up very upset that their mothers had no empathy and seemed to *not see* them at all. It created visible anxiety in the babies, and they concluded that this is one way that unhealthy relationships begin. That is how I have lived my entire life.

Love unreciprocated—you struggle, try to get a response. Oh my God, like I still do with my children, but I don't get it. I just wish that once, they would notice me. Notice that I'm teaching overseas, think it's cool, be proud of me. And maybe they are… but I haven't *received* praise. It makes one wonder whether you're loved at all. And even when you are loved, you can't feel it. You can't accept it. Thanks, Mom.

It's such a cluster of negative emotions:

- comparing self with others always leading to envy, anxiety, sadness.

- low self-esteem, never good enough, thin enough, smart enough.

- fear of abandonment—why would anyone love someone like me?

- disappointment with self. Oh my! The disappointment. I don't make enough money. Asked to teach in Europe, Australia. Why not every other freaking country in the world? What's wrong with me? Why don't I make enough money to travel wherever I want? Live wherever I want? And on and on and on with the disappointment and self-reprisal.

- negative self-talk. My therapist asked me what would happen if I talked to my patients like I do to myself in such a mean way. My response, "Of course not! For one thing, I wouldn't have any patients, would I?" Uh, exactly. But it's okay to belittle myself about everything. Self-evaluative ruminating, always negative, my "self" is flawed.

• and it's hard for me to take any criticism *at all*. It reminds me too much of being shamed in childhood and reinforces how inadequate I am.

Not feeling loved. Was that a Catholic thing? Never living up to expectations. How about that? One B on the report card wrecked the whole damn thing. Never getting any positive feedback like, "good for you for not being overweight like me." Or, "good grades, great job!" Is it possible that I felt that if I didn't live up to my parent's expectations, they wouldn't love me? I know that my mother wished at least one of her children, if not all of them, would be a doctor. Probably her lowest expectation was that we would go to college. Well, she got two doctors: I'm a Ph.D. and one of my brothers is a D.O. But I still always felt like that wasn't enough. I even told her once that I earned the highest degree in my field, Psychology, and my brother had earned the highest degree in his field, Osteopathy. But it didn't matter. I wasn't a "real" doctor. But who cares? It shouldn't matter what she thought. But boy, somehow it did. It still does.

Your Turn

Whew… so, how did your mother talk to you about your body if she talked to you about it at all?

How do *you* feel about your body? Did you make it through Catholic childhood unscathed regarding your body image?

Did you live up to her expectations, or was it impossible? Or didn't you care?

Oops, Pregnant and Not Married

YEAH, "IT" happened. After all the "men are disgusting" and "sex before marriage is a sin" lectures, I got pregnant before I was married. I was a freshman in college and only 18 years old. I'll spare you the details, but suffice it to say, not all birth control mechanisms work. All of my children are my pride, my joy, my loves, and two of the three were surprises due to birth control failures. In fact, my son loves to tell the story at parties about him being an IUD baby, and that we celebrate the notion my kids really wanted to have me as their mom. And I wouldn't have it any other way. When one of my daughters had difficulty getting pregnant, I was surprised because even when I was trying not to get pregnant, I did.

My advice: always, *always* be prepared for the pregnancy possibility. I wasn't prepared. What the hell was I going to do? At 18 I had to weigh:

> 1. telling my parents and doing what we did back then—go away to a home, have the baby, and give it up for adoption,

> 2. hiding the pregnancy and getting married, or

> 3. having an abortion (which wasn't really an option for me; I never would have done it).

I grew up in the days when abortion was illegal. I would have had to do some back-alley thing in another city, probably another state, maybe New York. I lived in Wilkes Barre, PA for God's sake. There was no doctor in WB doing abortions. And the idea of sticking a coat hanger into my uterus or taking some poisonous solution didn't appeal to me. Add to that the whole Catholic thing about abortion. There was a life in there and you were prohibited from ending that life. Plus, mortal sin, mortal sin, mortal sin. Send the baby's soul to Purgatory and mine straight to Hell. That's what an abortion would do. Bottom line, I *knew* there was a life in there, and I wasn't going to end it. Period.

Strange how things change and then go back. More and more constituencies trying to make it illegal again now.

So, I chose option 2. I just couldn't imagine telling my parents not only that I was sexually active, but that I didn't even know how to do that right. I got pregnant. What a disappointment I would be to them. It was horrible, just a horrible situation. And I was basically a kid. A kid who could only think of getting out of Wilkes Barre and becoming someone. Well, I was going to become *someone*: a mother. And I was going to have to take that terrifying step into the unknown without the support of my parents.

Part of my thinking in choosing the marriage option was that I was the only daughter, and I guess I felt like my parents would want their daughter to have a wedding. So, we planned a nice Catholic church ceremony. My family wasn't wealthy, and my engagement announcement was kind of a surprise. I'm sure my parents weren't saving for a wedding. It was probably strange for them that I dated for a few months, and then suddenly I'm so in love that I'm getting married. But it was what it was.

There were pre-Cana classes. What a pain. They lectured about family, intimacy, the rhythm method of birth control (too late), how to have a good fight and resolve it before bed, and even money matters.

The idea was that couples would have the opportunity to discuss important matters before they got married. All I cared about was getting the damn thing over with: hiding the truth and getting gone.

How awfully disappointed my parents must have felt. At 18 I'd be moving away. As I said, it was all I could think about my whole childhood, but not like this. My youngest brother, ten years younger than me, told me that my wedding day was one of the saddest days of his life. He couldn't believe that I was leaving him and my other brothers behind. He told me that if I thought things were bad before I left, they'd get worse after I left. Every time I think of him, I get teary eyed. I can't look at wedding pictures he's in without crying. I had no idea.

Naturally, all I could think of was making it through the wedding with no one knowing that I was pregnant. As I said earlier, I weighed about 98 pounds then, and, thank God, I hadn't gained much pregnancy weight before my wedding. I was able to get married in August without "showing."

Mom made my dress. As I said, we weren't wealthy. In fact, I thought we were poor. It was what some would call a smallish wedding and reception with a friend as the DJ. I left Wilkes Barre that night, the only place I knew. It was one of the saddest, scariest days of my life.

Your Turn

Did you have premarital sex?

Did you still live at home with your parents when you became sexually active?

What kind of wedding did you have if you're married?

The Apology Letter

IVING AWAY from the only home I'd known and, coincidentally, the one that I always said I couldn't wait to get away from, was miserable. I had this baby inside me—which was cool despite all the family craziness, *but* I was a *kid* in a place far away from my family. It was hard. Back then, in what I lovingly call "the good old days," the only communication I had with my family was letter writing and expensive long distance telephone calls. Yep, I'm *that* old. If it was up to me, I would have called home every day, but that cost too much. Then there was the elephant in the room… telling Mom and Dad that I was pregnant… over the phone. "Hi Mom and Dad. We are going to have a baby."

"Wow! When is this going to happen?"

"My due date is December 19."

Silence on the other end of the phone while they calculated how far away from our August 11 wedding day that was. I could hear their disappointment over the silent air waves.

Time for all hell to break loose; I guess it was more anger than disappointment. Tons of embarrassment too, I imagine. They demanded that I write an apology letter to them. That was my punishment. Being a pregnant teenager, making the hardest decision of my life on my own, and moving away to protect my parents. But all that wasn't punishment enough. I had to write them an apology letter. It would be another action in the long list of things I did to get my parents to love me, to accept me, to like me. At that moment, I knew I was the biggest disappointment of their lives. I was the cause of so much pain for them. I never reflected on the pain that they had caused me.

Because I was always trying to be the perfect child, I acknowledged my mistake and profusely apologized on the phone. Then came the letter writing, apologizing again. I asked them to forgive me for my mistake as sincerely as I could. And *I was sincere*. Afterall, *I wanted them to love me*, so if it meant begging for forgiveness, then I would have apologized until the cows came home. How was I ever going to get them to say they were proud of me now? I had completely blown that possibility.

You know what though, their behavior, their rejection of me, their anger, their disappointment… took away from the beautiful little girl that was growing inside of me. They rejected both of us. Look at this picture of us—one of my favorites. Look at this sweetness that they couldn't even perceive because of their own prejudices.

My parents rejected their first grandchild, *my* first child, because of their own feelings. Damn… could they have been less selfish or cruel? I mentioned earlier that I was going to have to take this huge step into the unknown without the support of my parents and there it was: their rejection and being asked to write an apology letter to them.

I've been practicing Chinese medicine for over 20 years and understand the impact of prenatal emotions on the fetus. That knowledge makes me feel awful for my firstborn and what she had to go through during my pregnancy while she was in my body. That was the time when she should have felt calm and secure, getting all the nutrients she needed. Her job was to float around, be nurtured, feel loved. But I'm certain that she could feel my anxiety, my sadness, my grief, the surprise of that pregnancy. Every mother's worst fear is your child thinking he or she is unwanted. I've probably spent her entire life feeling guilty about that, trying to make it up to her, figuring out how to have her know how much I love her, wishing it had been different. *And wanting her to love me.* Being a *bad* mother is a top fear too, and I started right from her conception with that one. Shock, fear, worry, sadness, more worry, more fear, all while she was growing in my womb.

There it is again—I wanted her/them to love me. That freaking thing has followed me along on my journey with my children. *My biggest fear is that my children won't love me*, that they'll abandon me, that I won't have good relationships with them. *That* is what drives all my behavior with them. All my behavior in my life… trying to make them proud of me, trying to make them notice me, trying to make them care. Forty-nine plus years of it, and I'm tired. Don't get me wrong, I love them and my grandchildren more than anything. But I know that some of my "I have to be the perfect mother for you" is partially driven by my fear that they won't love me.

Maybe I need to forgive myself.

Your Turn

Did you ever do anything that you felt humiliated your parents, even though it was maybe just something that happened? Or was the result of a bad decision?

Did you ever feel like your parents would never forgive you for something?

Raising My Children as Catholics

THE KIDS' dad and I were both Catholics, albeit "ambiguous Catholics," and it seemed like a no brainer that our children would be Catholics. It sounds weird even today saying, "would *be* Catholics." I spent a good part of growing up saying that I would not be like my mother/parents. I would not raise my children in the same way. But maybe that was about not letting their father hit them with the belt like mine did or not saying the proper words for body parts or not talking about body functions at all. It was going to be different for my children. They were going to be allowed to have opinions. We were going to talk about body parts and sex and maybe even walk around braless.

Don't get me wrong. I've always considered myself a Catholic and say I'm a Catholic if asked. I belong to a parish and my business donates monthly to the church's food pantry. We occasionally go to Mass. But I'm a critical thinker, a Research Psychologist who tries to think rationally about religion as well as be open to everything. I guess thats why I call myself an "ambiguous Catholic," more *spiritual* than a member of an organized flock.

And there's the sin thing. I hated the idea of teaching my children about sins. For God's sake, their mother had committed one of the biggest sins ever: premarital sex. How could I expect them to know that about me and then not sin themselves? I wanted to teach them how to be good, kind people without the threat of the mortal, "you're-going-to-Hell," sin thing. I just wasn't going to do that to them. There were important lessons though: learn about God, learn about being a good person, learn about not hurting others, learn to love and accept yourself. Lots and lots of lessons. Like how I used to monitor their television viewing so they wouldn't learn unacceptable behaviors. They used to hate it when I would watch cartoons with them and comment on the violence. When Daffy Duck's head got blown off by a shotgun but immediately grew back, I'd tell them that in real life the person's head would stay blown off. He'd be dead. They hated that. But I hated violence and wanted my children to be non-violent. I had studied aggression for my Master's thesis and learned the hopelessness of stopping aggression and violence in society. So that was part of my nagging. In real life you can't shoot people, punch people, etc. and expect that they would be well. Check out old time cartoons; they're terribly violent.

All of my children were baptized, and I made a big deal of it for my parents. Made certain that my parents knew they were being baptized. Made sure they knew we were purifying them of Original Sin and ushering them into the Catholic Church.

There wasn't a hyper-focus on naming each one after a saint. Honestly, if it happened, I think it was more happenstance than anything else. Naturally, I couldn't name them something like *Jazznique*. My mom would need to approve. My oldest was named Audrey Michele. No saint Audrey it turns out, but her namesake is actually St. Ethelreda, the patron saint of throat complaints. Michele means *gift from God*. I love that. Next came Jennifer Rene. There is no St. Jennifer but there is a St. René, patron saint of Canada of all things. And then came Brian Patrick. There's not really a St. Brian, but of course we all know about St. Patrick, the patron saint of Ireland. And my father's middle name was Patrick so there was that one and only reference to anything

Lucas family. Funny though, mom's name was *Elsie Jean*—not a very Catholic name. It's a wonder how John and Mary Braxtor, devout Catholics, named one of their girls Elsie Jean. By the time mom was born and named, Elsie the cow was a popular mean thing to call girls named Elsie, so she hated her name. I can understand.

I wanted my children to have popular names, names they would hopefully like—because, of course, *I wanted them to love me*. Giving them a name they would hate would create an untenable situation. I guess we were lucky that the priest didn't intervene since the names weren't saints' names per se. Clearly, I felt pressured to at least start my children off as Catholics to please my parents, so the poor kids had to endure First Confession and First Communion as well.

Your Turn

Why do you feel that your parents raised you as a Catholic? Were they devout or was it "just the way it was?"

If you have children, did you raise them as Catholics?

Are you still all practicing Catholics?

JMJ

My D I V O R C E

NATURALLY, I was taught that marriage is for life. If you got divorced, you weren't allowed to remarry unless the first marriage was annulled. You could be divorced in the "eyes of the state" but not in the "eyes of God." It's because God joins the couple in marriage. Yes, God is there at your wedding, securing your vows. The vows are between the couple and God himself. I'd say, "or herself" but we're talking back in the 70s, so I'll go with the feeling of that day: God *is* male.

Anyway, I got divorced when the kids were about 2, 3, and 6. We had a regular dad goes to work and mom (me) stays home life, but I wanted what I called "freedom." Their father was a good guy, hard worker, but I wanted to finish college and not just be a stay-at-home mom. I wanted to help stop the nuclear power plant, Marble Hill from being built across the river from where we lived.

The kids and I moved out of the house, and visitation was set up. I enrolled at the University of Louisville and got a job with a group called The Senate of Religious. One day I was telling my boss, Sister Mary Claire, that the kids and I needed a place to live. Lo and behold, she knew of an empty rectory—of all places—that the pastor of the parish would rent to us for very low rent. He was willing to do that because there was a group of retired ladies who played Bingo in the large front parlor once a month. He wanted the rectory to have some life in it, some cleanliness in it, so it was ours. But what a spot! It was a mess! My brother John—God love him—came down for a few weeks to clean up the place for us. He literally hosed down the first floor. Really, he took a garden hose and washed it from ceilings to floor. We put a roach bomb in the kitchen and came home to a sheet of roaches covering every appliance. *Ugh*. But it had an enormous kitchen, living room, three bedrooms, multiple bathrooms, and even an office where I could study.

Across the parking lot were our neighbors, the Sisters of Charity, living in their convent. On the other side of the rectory was the church of St. John Vianney with a little yard with a statuary fountain in between. We didn't even know who St. John Vianney was. Turns out he's the patron saint of parish priests and was ardently devoted to the Blessed Virgin Mary and the sacrament of confession. They say he would spend twelve hours a day hearing confessions, sometimes more.

It's probably easy to guess where my kids ended up attending school. Yep, uniforms and all. Sounds like I didn't hold to the idea that my children's childhoods were going to be different than mine. There they were in Catholic grade school, doing all the usual and customary Catholic grade school things. *Sigh*.

Despite all the travails, it worked out. All my children are happily married, have good jobs or the opportunity not to work because their spouse has a great job and income, and have children I adore. They all have college degrees, although Brian is the only one who actually uses his degree in his career. At least they all had the university experience. I can't help feeling that I did some damage by choosing to go out on my own while they were so young.

After living with parents like mine, who clearly didn't love each other—or at least Mom didn't love Dad, at all—I just didn't want to do that to my children. Back then, there I was: a young person, more or less on my own, making a life-changing decision. So, I made it.

Fodder for therapy—for me and for my children I imagine. That I regret sometimes. I wish they could have had a "leave it to Beaver" childhood, but I can't go back. All I can do is spend my life trying to make it up to them in any way I know how. Remember, *I want them to love me.*

Despite Mom's opinion about divorce, she told me once that she wished she had divorced my dad. Oh my!

Did that sound like she thought I did the right thing?

Did that sound like she understood me?

Did that sound like she was proud of a decision that I'd made?

Were we actually having a woman-to-woman moment?

Regardless, I was shocked that she would say that. Her, the devout Catholic who went to Mass everyday, basically telling me she wished she was divorced.

Funny the things that we remember.

Your Turn

What do you think would be better, living with parents who don't get along or with those who are divorced?

Actually, "better" is a good word—how about healthier?

Did you grow up in a divorced family?

What is your opinion of getting remarried after divorce?

Dating and Remarriage: To Annul or Not to Annul

TWENTY SOMETHINGS date. So I did. In my mind, I can't apologize or punish myself enough for not being at home with my children every minute that I wasn't at work or in school. Did you say Catholic guilt? Oh, I'm an expert at that. I was guilty then and I'm still guilty. I will never make it up to them for their worse than average childhood, but I keep trying. More fodder for therapy.

Some ten years after I got divorced, I met my current husband. I told my parents that I had had my first marriage annulled, so it was "okay" in the eyes of God for me to get married again. What a bunch of bull.

And here's one more crazy, bullshit thing. My husband and I slept in separate rooms while my parents were in town for our wedding. We pretended we were practicing celibacy for my parents. We were lying. One might say we did that so my parents wouldn't be uncomfortable with us sleeping in the same bed in their presence. Or, you could say that I still wanted my parents to love me, to accept me, to think I was a good person. *I was still trying to be someone they could be proud of.* As a single mother, I had raised children who all turned out okay, earned a doctorate degree, and taught at the university level, but still I felt as if it wasn't enough. Nothing would ever be enough. It would have been so nice to hear "good job" or "we're so proud of you" just once. I still wish my children would say that too… talk about being damaged goods.

Wishing that your parents loved you or were proud of you isn't a Catholic thing per se, right? But trying to live up to the standards of good Catholic parents *is* a Catholic guilt thing. The pressure to be perfect, the pressure to be good, the pressure not to sin. And it seems sometimes that everything you do is a sin. Have sex outside of marriage. Lie to your parents. Get married again without having your first marriage annulled. Skip out on Mass every Sunday. Lying about that too. Even when we went to Moab, we'd tell my parents we had gone to Mass at the local Church. It never ends. Well, it did when my parents died, although there are still the damaging remnants of my entire life before they died.

Your Turn

As an adult, did you lie to your parents about your non-Catholic behavior?

Did you feel like they *knew* anyway?

Did you ever get over the idea that they were somehow watching you?

How did you get over your guilt about lying to them? All you were trying to do was have a regular life.

When Did You Start to Become an Ambiguous Catholic?

THIS IS a hard one to answer. It implies the "when" of my beginning to doubt what I was being taught. It implies the "when" of my not wanting to go to church every Sunday… to go to confession every week… to have to wear a dress to Mass… to have to wear a hat to Mass… to have to schedule not eating so I could receive communion… to go to Catholic high school, etc., etc., ad nauseam.

I can start with grade school. I knew then that I didn't want to go to Catholic high school. Was that because I thought Catholicism was bull? Not certain, but I knew I was done with nuns, uniforms, Mass on every freaking Catholic holiday and Sundays, and especially feeling like I was constantly doing something wrong, which equates to sinning. Maybe it started with those fake confessions I made up every week in grade school after receiving my First Confession. I *knew* I was lying to the priest each week; I was making up sins so he would have something to forgive. I was *doing penance* for sins I didn't commit. I was just following orders. I confessed, received a blessing, and followed orders about how many and which prayers to say. The priest pronounced, "Say one Our Father and three Hail Marys."

Somewhere, in one of Matthew's gospels, Jesus said something to the effect of, when you pray, don't be like a hypocrite. Well, I was 7 years old and felt like a hypocrite when I'd make up sins for confession every week. It didn't matter that I was told that penance is a virtue... like I even understood what being virtuous was. I had no idea that I was living up to the high moral standards of the Catholic Church and living up to their ideal of goodness. *Sheesh*.

But who knows, maybe that's why I've always been what one would call a "good person." I do my best:

- not to break rules,

- not to break laws,

- not to hurt other people,

- not to give in to inappropriate urges,

- to always do the right thing,

- to act according to values and principles,

- to live an ethical life,

- to train my children and their children not to break rules, not to break laws, not to hurt other people, so the beat goes on.

It's funny that I've read that *truth is the highest virtue.* Yet, forcing me to go to confession every week basically forced me to not live up to the highest virtue of all.

Nobody should be forced to live a lie.

Your Turn

How long did you live a lie?

Or were your parents understanding enough to accept your religious views if they differed from yours?

Or were you brave enough to live the life you wanted?

Banned Books, Mom, and George

PPARENTLY, MY mother didn't know that the Catholic Church gave up the *Index of Forbidden Books* (*Index Librorum Prohibitorum*) in the 1960s. Well, "gave up" isn't exactly correct. They stopped publishing it and at that point it became a historic document. Honestly, they never banned books per se, but did compile a list of books whose content they felt was problematic. It was good old-fashioned control of the press under the guise of preventing the spread of heresy. The "powers that be" didn't want us Catholics getting any ideas about doubting the Church, especially its authority, questioning our religion, or abandoning the religious practices they had taught us. They thought that books, other people's ideas, might contaminate our faith. There were even some versions of *The Bible* that were banned. No kidding. No thinking allowed.

Remember, I grew up in bra burning, women's liberation times. I recall reading about a book or a paper called *The Gospel of Mary*. I thought it was so cool, *but* it was never included in *The Bible* or ever really talked about. It's a pretty obscure thing to even know exists. Why? Well, one theory is that the Church is so patriarchal that there was no way that a document, any document, written by a woman was going to be included in something like *The Bible*. It has also been opined that it had some allusions to the fact that women should be included in decision making, that we should be allowed to participate in Church rituals, and basically was a pro-feminism commentary. Those of us who still read the books, without permission, could have been excommunicated. It makes me laugh to write that. Excommunicated for reading a book. And you know that excommunication from the Roman Catholic Church equated to eternal spiritual damnation. I probably just barely escaped eternal damnation by even mentioning *The Gospel of Mary.*

Books could have been banned for sexual or coarse language, or for having ideas that might lead to the corruption of the morals of Catholics. Again, no thinking allowed. Talk about control freaks. I, and you, can read something, anything, and make up our own minds about it! Someone can write that Jesus and Peter were the first ever Nazis, and I can take it or leave it. I can believe it or not. But Mom, *oh my*. As far as she was concerned, *you do not read a banned book.* Remember, the church did not ban books. They had a list of books they didn't like because they wanted the morals of Catholics to stay intact. They didn't want us doubting the dogma. They didn't want any thinking going on or questioning the "fact" that the religious practices they had taught us were important for our spiritual good. Better to not know other points of view, other facts, other ideas, or that other religions exist; otherwise, we risk our trip to heaven.

I'll never forget the one time Mom was visiting us and she saw that my husband George had been reading the book *The Last Temptation of Christ.* Wow! Did that book cause a stir. She confronted George about reading it and reminded him that it was a banned book. That means, according to her thinking, he was banned from reading it. George told her that he had the intelligence enough to read anything and then make decisions based on his other knowledge, life experience, beliefs, etc. And that it was silly to think he had to be told what was appropriate to read. Mom was furious! It was winter, but she walked right out the door and sat on the front porch in order to be away from him.

Her daughter was married to a heretic, for God's sake. A free-thinking man, and she couldn't take it. Honestly, I think it was probably the Jesus being tempted by sex part of the book that hurt her sensibilities the most. It seems silly to me. The book basically portrayed Christ as a human with human desires, human doubts, human temptations, but he was more perfect than that in her eyes.

So, the book was banned.

Your Turn

Did your parents have books you weren't allowed to read?

What do you think of book banning? Is it scary to you, or do you think it's necessary?

What banned books have you read?

Death and Catholicism

DAD DIED four months to the day after the doctor told him he would die if he did nothing to treat the liver cancer. He avoided the necessary surgeries and any treatment. I remember the date that he died because we got the "you have about four months to live if you do nothing" news on my birthday, April 12, and he died on August 12. The doctor told Dad he wasn't the best candidate for surgery. I hated his doctor for saying that because Dad was only 77, and I thought he had more life to live. I wanted him to live. But he was ready to die. Actually, he had been ready to die for ten years since he had the major stroke. It had paralyzed him on his right side in the prime of retired life: 66 years old. His body was still alive, but he was dead inside. His soul died on the day of that stroke. I tried to make him happy to be alive. Me… *the fixer*. I called every day to check on him, and to say I loved him to counter him saying, "I wish I didn't wake up today." I'd tell him, "But Dad, we love you. You have people who love you. You want to see your grandkids grow up." Like I said, I wanted him to live.

Mom hated the whole post-stroke thing, hated him, hated that he needed help. She would do things like begrudgingly make him a sandwich before she left for the day and let him know how unhappy she was. A real angry housewife. It was very sad.

I was heartbroken when Dad died. I wrote and gave the eulogy because my brothers had no use for my father. They told me that I had no idea how bad it had gotten after I left. If I thought it was bad when I lived there, I guess their lives were even more miserable after I left. Dad had this thing where he would call my brothers "nothings." He would literally point to each one and say, "Nothing. Nothing. Nothing. Nothing," and then point to himself and say, "Something." That didn't happen to me, so I was happy to talk kindly about my father at his funeral. Eulogies are always nice; you never get up there and talk about how awful the person was. I even talked about Dad changing diapers, which Mom told me he did. After all the years of her telling me how awful he was, she shared *that* memory.

Shortly after the funeral, I had a dream that Dad and I met in a church, and he was a much younger man. Maybe our human bodies rejuvenate after death. Or as Mom believed, maybe when we meet each other in our bodies at the end of the world, we will all have young, strong, healthy bodies.

Mom lived about 5 years of freedom after Dad died. She had a little apartment and a cat named Ginger. She taught private music lessons and continued volunteering at the Pro-life Center. Then one day she was dead: pulmonary embolism, suffered while she was on the phone with her last living sister. Thank God for that, or who knows how long she would have lay dead and rotting in her apartment before someone noticed. Another blessing is that one of my brothers lived near Mom and was able to be there to deal with the immediate aftermath of her death.

My daughter Audrey and I immediately flew up to Wilkes Barre to deal with everything. Audrey was my rock. After the first night she said, "Mom, you must be exhausted… you were up all night crying." But I wasn't. I was so shocked and sad that I apparently cried even during my sleep.

Another Catholic funeral coming up. We got Mom's students to do the music, one adopted her cat Ginger, and one of my brothers wrote and gave the eulogy. Her funeral was well attended because of her teaching and volunteering; she was pretty well known in the small community that was Wilkes Barre. I remember sobbing out loud while her students were playing music, and when it stopped I heard myself. Naturally, I stopped immediately because we just don't do that. We don't sob out loud so everyone can hear our heartbreak. Makes them too uncomfortable, I guess. Never mind about the person whose mother dropped dead a week before. I wasn't supposed to make other people uncomfortable.

Before the funeral came the cleanup. Her apartment was full. We sent bags and bags of stuff to the parish and Goodwill. Then there was the dining room table where she kept junk mail. There was a mountain of it. She kept ads that had return envelopes so she could use it to send back pro-life propaganda instead of the membership form that the advertisers were expecting. I despised that practice of hers. We talked about it for years. How rude, how awful I thought it was, but she kept doing it. I told her that some poor secretary who had lost a baby could open that envelope, see the anti-abortion literature, and be traumatized. But she didn't care. She had to get her Pro-life message out.

My brothers and I gathered her stuff for each of us to take home if we wanted. As I said, we were poorish, so the stuff amounted to Christmas decorations, costume jewelry, Mom's JFK collection, nothing worth anything except sentimentally. But still it led to lively discussions. As the oldest, I decided we would put everything in a pile and hand it out: 1, 2, 3, 4, 5. Each of us would randomly get the stuff. A blank dance card ended up in my pile. One of my brothers wanted to trade me for it. It was a blank piece of paper. I responded, "Take it, please. I don't want to trade. Just take it." Yeah… families after death. I don't think it ever goes smoothly and without any hard feelings. Then that was it; both of my parents were gone but their messages live on. Have I said it before? That's what therapy is for: to deal with, live with, get over those freaking messages.

But I wish they had lived longer. I have bunches of patients who are my age and whose parents are alive, or at least one is alive. I envy that. I tell people that my parents died young because I *do* think that 76 and 77 are young. Too young to be dead. I have a four-generation picture of my mother's mother, my mother, me, and my daughter Audrey. I had always imagined that I would be in another four-generation picture. It would be my mother, me, one of my children, and their child—my grandchild. But Mom didn't make it long enough for that to happen. My hope is to still have a four-generation picture. This one will be of me, my child, their child, and my grandchild's child. Yep, planning to be a great-grandmother!

Your Turn

Are your parents still living? What is your relationship with them like?

Do they have a funeral plan? Are their affairs in order?

Do you talk about it with them?

What Now?

S o here we are. We are the age that we are. We have lived through what we've lived through and are where we are in our lives. To say that we were traumatized seems somehow to be too much, too dramatic. But when it fits, it fits.

Trauma is a strong, scary word. But honestly, my childhood experience drives my animal brain to think that if one of our appliances breaks, we're going to go bankrupt. My go to emotion is fear and the worst possible outcome. All those years of sitting on the steps, waiting for my dad to come home safe, thinking of the absolute worst thing that could happen to most kids, a parent dying, has left its mark. I was a worried, scared, helpless, poor kid. And that's the message that my amygdala, my animal brain, transmits throughout my body all the time. Sometimes I wonder how I would be different if I had been nurtured through that worry. How would I be different if my mother had soothed me somehow that Dad would be home, not to worry? Hugged me. But that never happened. For one thing, I snuck out of my room after she went to bed. As far as I know, she had no idea that I sat on the steps every night. She had no idea that I worried, waited for him to come up the stairs, and then could go to bed. I must have been flat out exhausted as a kid.

According to both modern medicine and Chinese medicine—my

career is a combination of both—our lungs hold grief. They don't work well if we're holding on to grief. And we need a healthy breathing cycle in order to have a strong immune system. No wonder I had asthma. My twenty-plus years of practicing Chinese medicine has also shown me that I've inherited my father's fear. DNA is energy; we inherit the energies of our parents, our grands, our great grands, on and on. We are helpless not to inherit it. Dad's father ran off and his mother committed suicide when he was five, leaving him abandoned, alone. *So,* there's that inherited part of my rat brain, even older than my sitting on the stairs, hoping he'd come home alive.

That's my legacy; yours is hopefully different.

I'm certain that you and I have experienced some of the same things as Catholic daughters of Catholic mothers, or even Jewish daughters of Jewish mothers, or Lutheran daughters of Lutheran mothers. The question is "what now?" Here are a few suggestions:

- Find a Chinese medicine practitioner who specializes in healing trauma patterns. That's my specialty, and like they say, healers get into their profession to heal themselves. Practitioners like me often do distance treatments, so you don't even have to be present to be healed.

- Find a good psychologist or other type of therapist.

- Do cranial sacral work to break energetic patterns.

- Try EMDR, which is a very effective therapy for some trauma.

- Run, run, run: aerobic exercise soothes the emotional brain. Exercise is like a magic pill for depression, anxiety, insomnia, weight issues, and more.

• Pray. I just lit a candle to the Blessed Mother today for a family issue. Oh, and recite one to the Holy Spirit too, asking him to enlighten the parties involved.

• Breathe. One of my favorite breathing methods, the one that I suggest to my patients, is to breathe deeply from the belly up. Yes, belly up. Your belly will expand when you breathe deeply. Bring your breath up and then start the exhale from the top of your chest down to the belly. It's circular. Bottom up… top down. It gets you into your body and out of your animal brain.

• One thing I'm working on is to stop apologizing, apologizing, apologizing. Oh my God! Everything on the Thanksgiving table isn't the same warmth. Apologize. One person doesn't like a dish. Apologize. A gift is the wrong size. Apologize *and* feel embarrassed on top of that. Things don't have to be perfect! Life isn't black and white, perfect or awful. That's the message I got when I was young, but it's not real life. In our house, you were good or bad, right or wrong. Well, we weren't allowed to express our opinions, so we never had an opportunity to be wrong. When I became a strutter at football games—what we now call pom pom girls or those on a dance squad—I'll never forget that my mother said, "One asthma attack, one cold, and you're off the squad." And then there was the need to achieve straight As or your schoolwork is unacceptable. There it is. No chances. No colds or you're off the squad. No B's or you'll be studying more. Black and white: no chances or room for error. Life isn't like that. I'm not perfect and everything I do does *not* have to be perfect.

• Listen to chanting or chant yourself. One of the best, most meditative experiences I've ever had in my life was when I attended chanting events at the Nityananda Institute in Portland, Oregon. It was powerful.

• And guess what? Studies show that talking with a trusted other is often enough to calm down your rat brain. It calms your amygdala: gets you out of the fear response, gets your brain out of the alarm stage. You don't even have to have a conversation. The logical part of your brain, the "I'm safe now" part, just needs you to talk with someone you trust. Just talk. I have patients who text me and say, "My amygdala just needs to talk," and then they tell me their story. I do the same thing with a friend of mine. The *Denver Amygdala Calming Group!*

• Savor the good things. Taking a trip for example. First, savor the planning. It's fun, right? Think about where you are going to go, who you are going with, the fun things you are going to do, and savor it. Then there's the enjoying part: living the trip, living the vacation, living the experience. Joy, joy, joy! Finally, the third part is to relive the moment, relive the joy through memories and photos. My husband is the perfect savorer. He does all three steps every time.

Me? I'm more of a crier when I look at pictures. Therapy is helping me realize, while there is a sadness that accompanies living in an empty nest, I did joyful things with the ones I love. We had fun, and those are happy memories. Those are memories to be smiled about. That's reliving the joy.

• Stop trying to fix everything and everyone. I used to wish that I could fix my parent's marriage. So, guess what that set me up for? For trying to make everything right… every little thing, every event.

• Laugh. Laughter has been studied as "good medicine." It relieves stress and triggers healthy physical and emotional changes in your body, including boosting your immune system.

• Write. A good time to end with your final question for your journal.

Your Turn

What is perfect anyway?

About the Author

Dr. Martha Lucas holds a Ph.D. in Research Psychology as well as her degree in Chinese Medicine. Lucas has more than 20 years of teaching and speaking experience and is described as "a dynamic speaker who keeps her classes engaged and who can explain complex information in an understandable way." She teaches courses worldwide. Her private practice is based in Denver, Colorado where she specializes in internal medicine.

Besides Catholic Daughters of Catholic Mothers: A Memoir and Guided Journal, her books include *Pulse Diagnosis: Beyond Slippery and Wiry*, *Cosmetic Acupuncture Works!*, *The Mei Zen Cosmetic Acupuncture Workbook*, and *You Don't Need Botox* (out of print). Her latest book project is for children and includes: *The Skeleton in a Tutu Gets Acupuncture* and others in pre-production. She has also written countless published articles.

www.acupuncturewoman.com

About the Publisher

ArmLin House is a publisher and production company. We publish your media or help you do it yourself. We can produce your sellable media or create your marketing images and videos. With over thirty years of experience, our team can write, design, and handle the technical details to bring your product to market.

ArmLin House, Inc.
P.O. Box 2522
Littleton, Colorado 80161-2522
contact@armlinhouse.com
www.armlinhouse.com

www.ingramcontent.com/pod-product-compliance
Lightning Source LLC
Chambersburg PA
CBHW071008120626
46546CB00003B/987